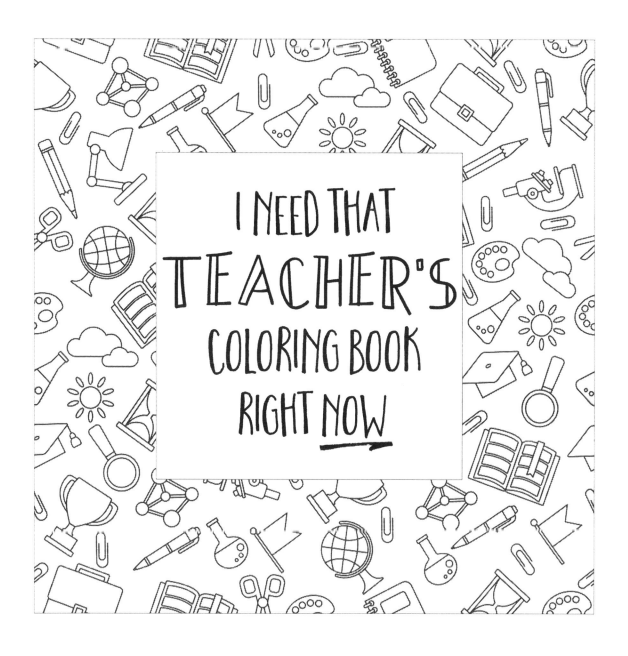

I NEED THAT TEACHER'S COLORING BOOK RIGHT NOW

By Jim Erskine

Published by
Arf! Arf! Studios

I NEED THAT TEACHER'S COLORING BOOK RIGHT NOW

Arf! Arf! Studios
PO Box 1187
Canmer, KY 42722
(say what?)

Search for Arf Arf Studios on Amazon
for more great creative books!

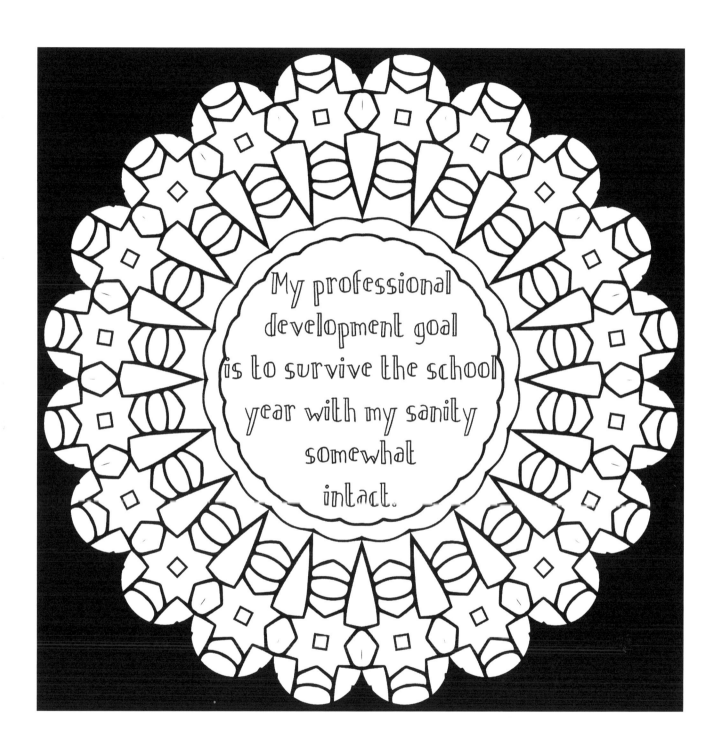

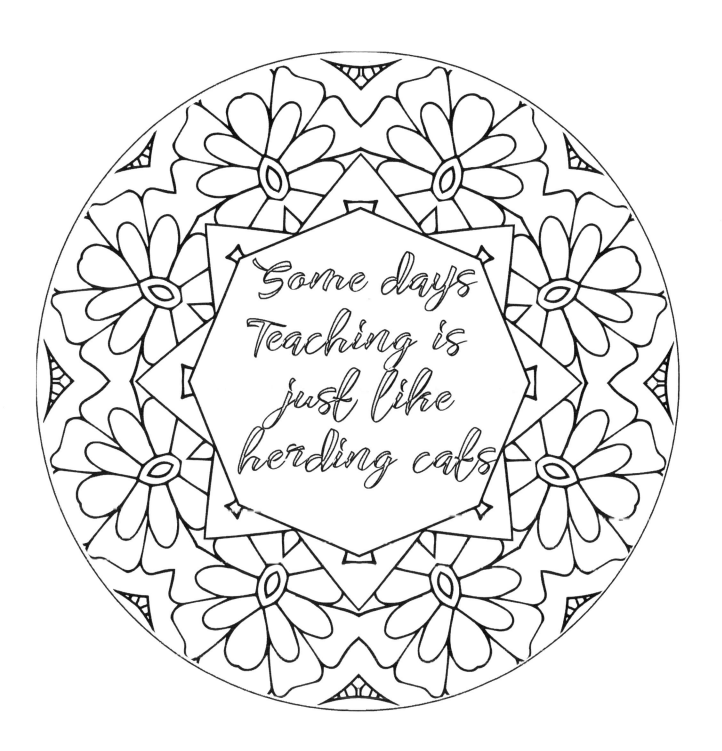

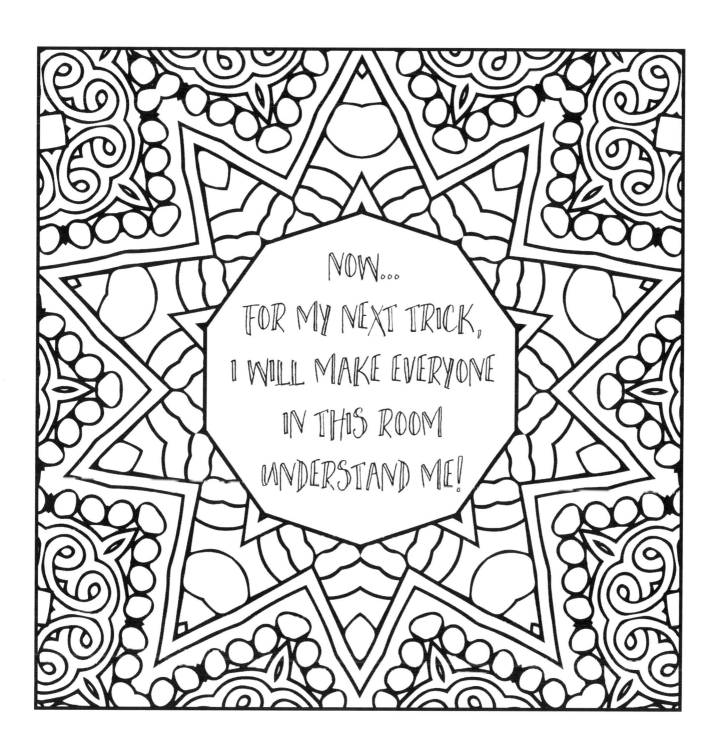

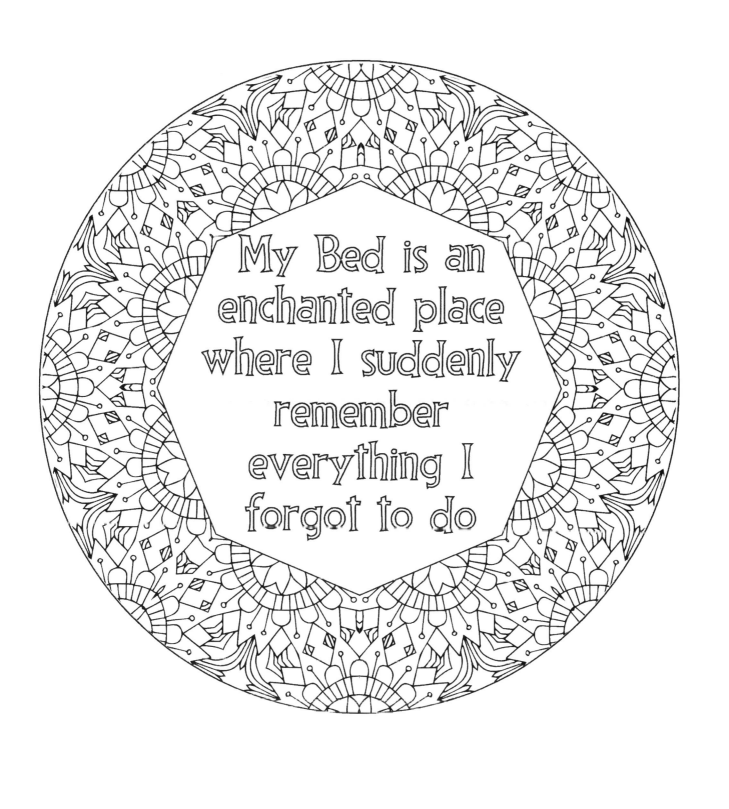

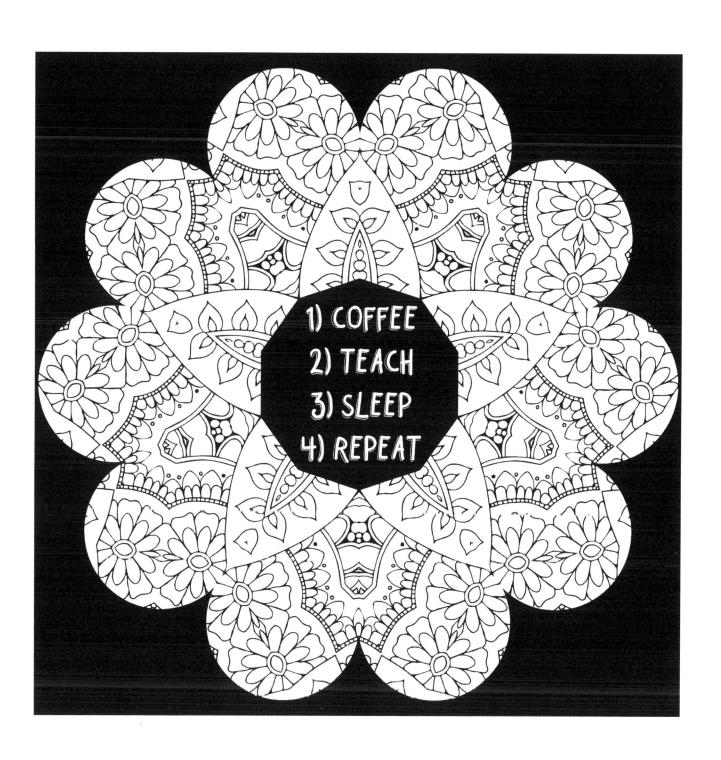

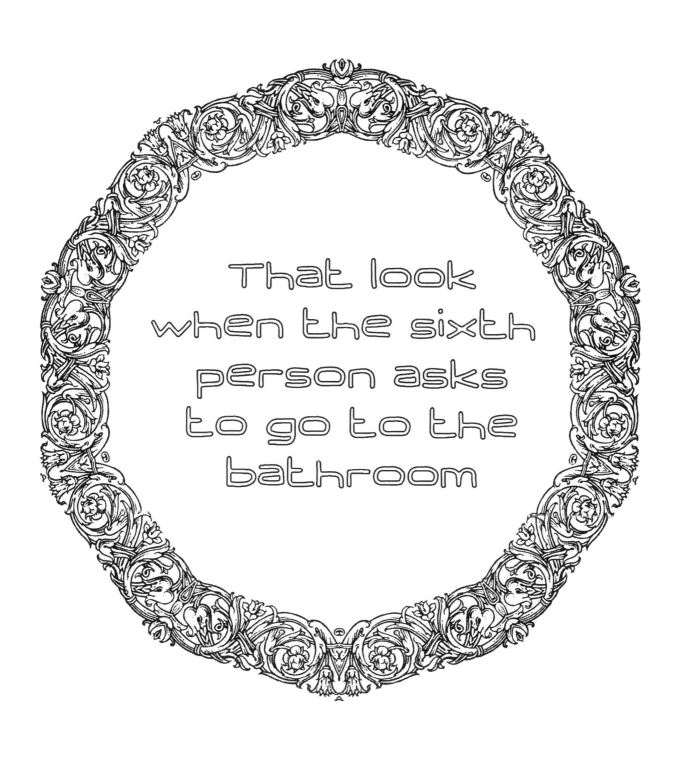

That look
when the sixth
person asks
to go to the
bathroom

I'm just going to

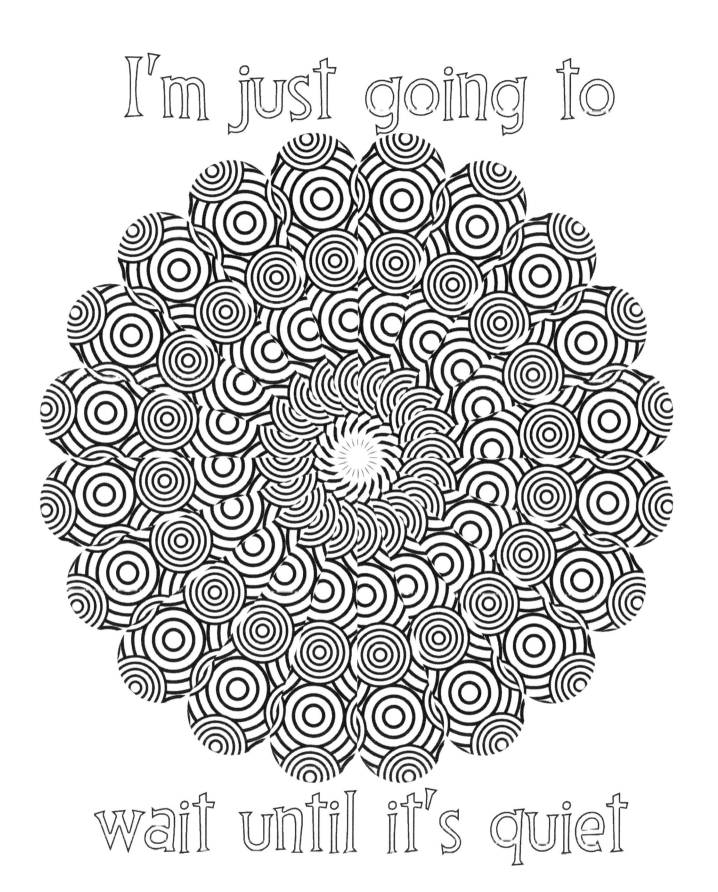

wait until it's quiet

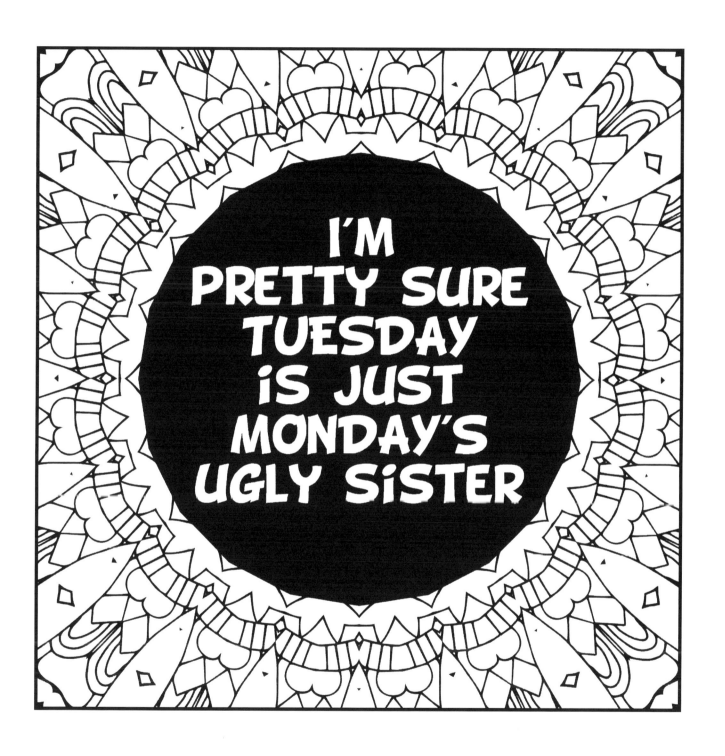

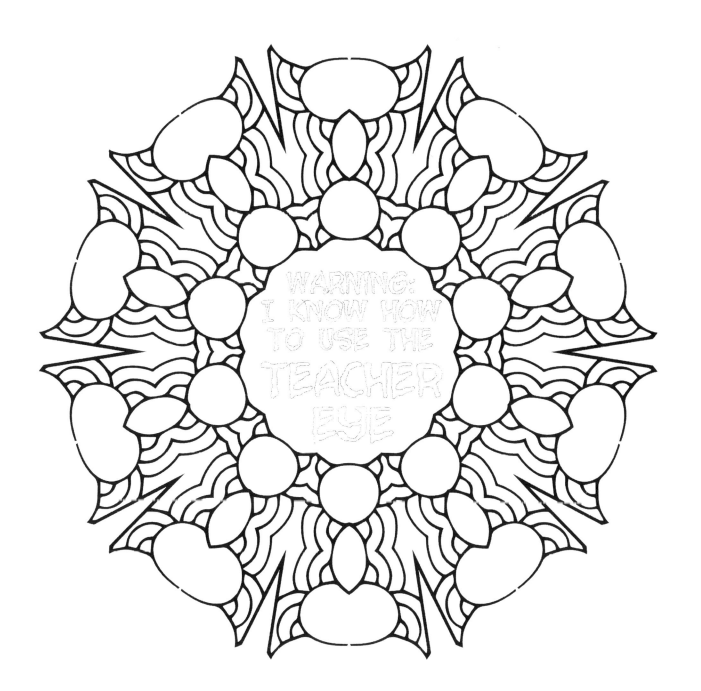

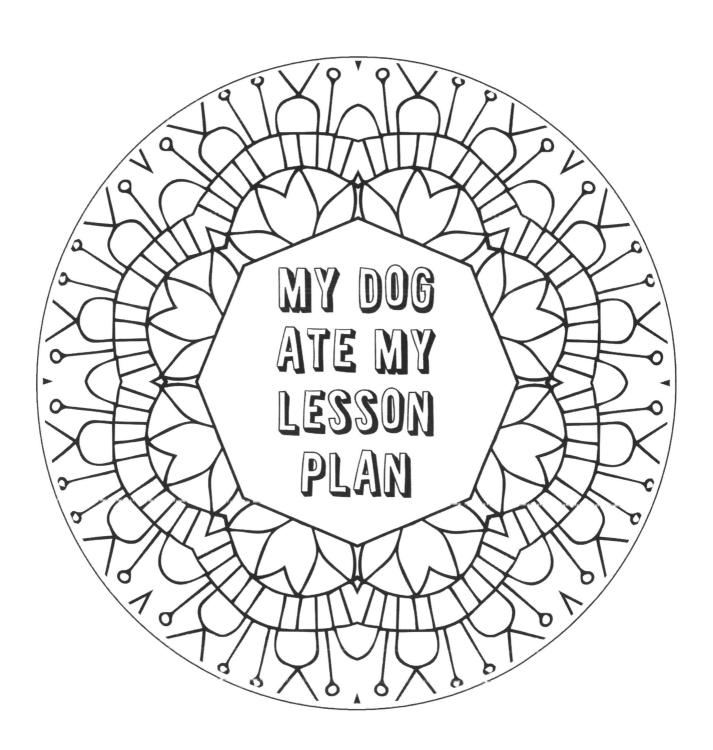

JUST LOOK
AT ALL THOSE
PAPERS I DIDN'T
GRADE OVER
BREAK

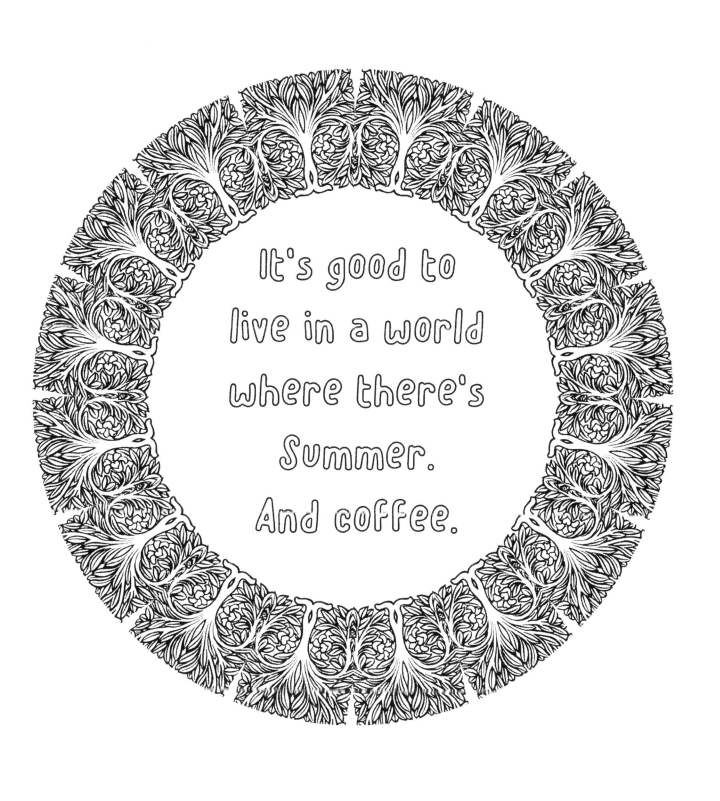

It's good to
live in a world
where there's
Summer.
And coffee.

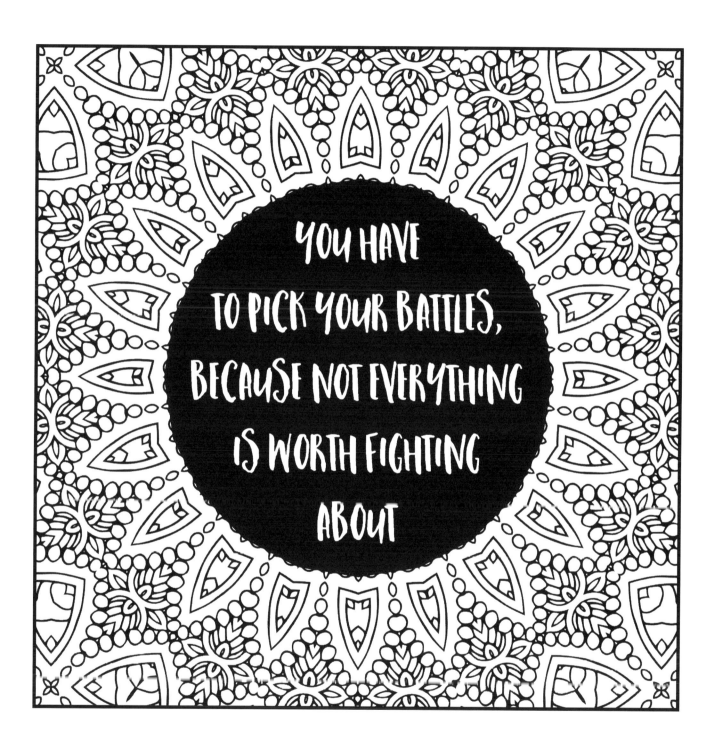

YOU HAVE TO PICK YOUR BATTLES, BECAUSE NOT EVERYTHING IS WORTH FIGHTING ABOUT

I will not yell.
I will not have
a temper tantrum.
I will not tease
the other kids.

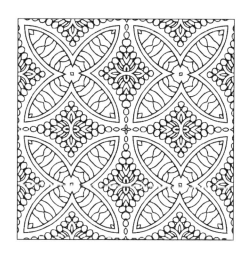

I will be good
because
I am the teacher.

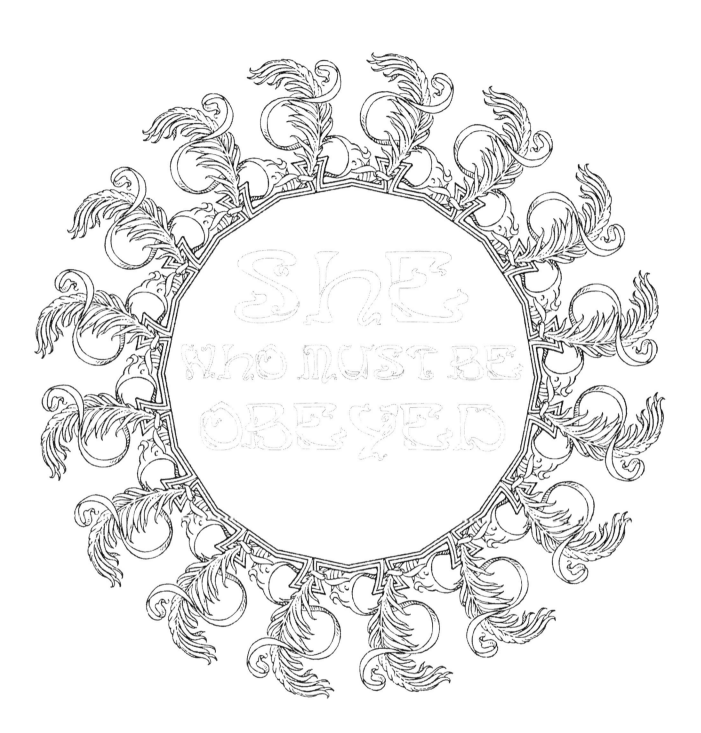

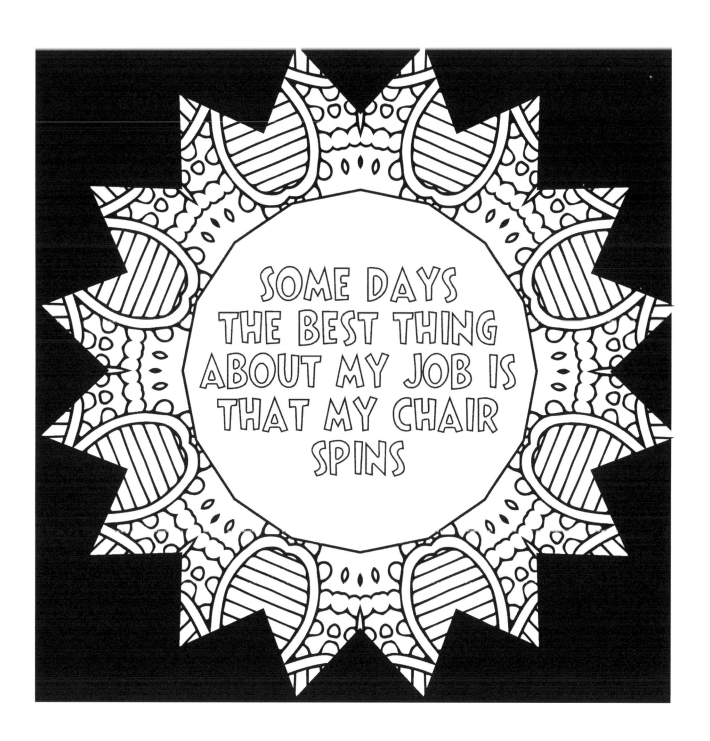

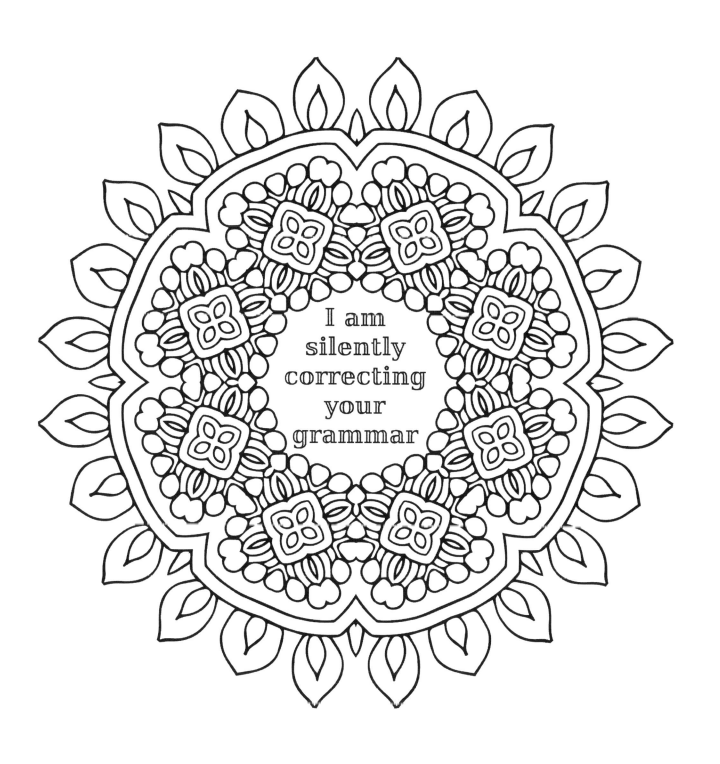

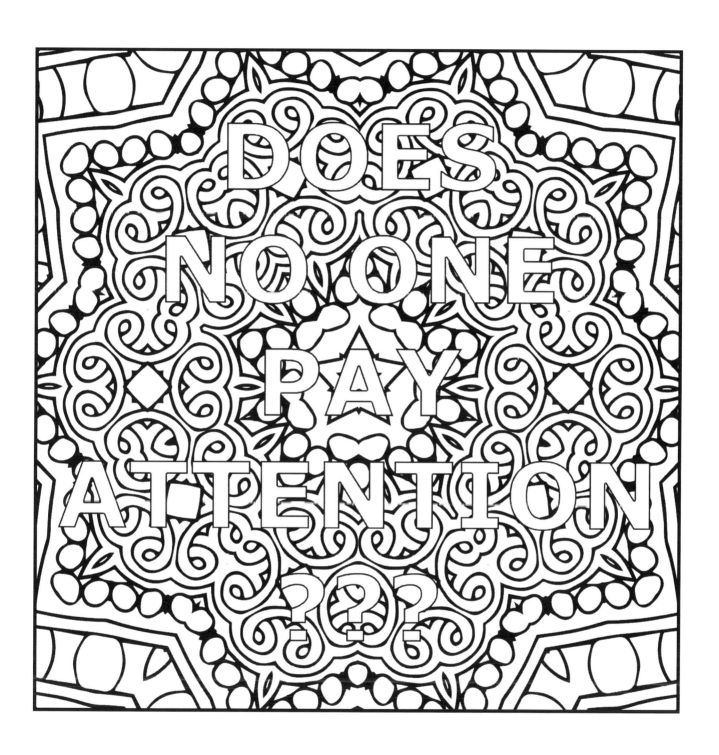

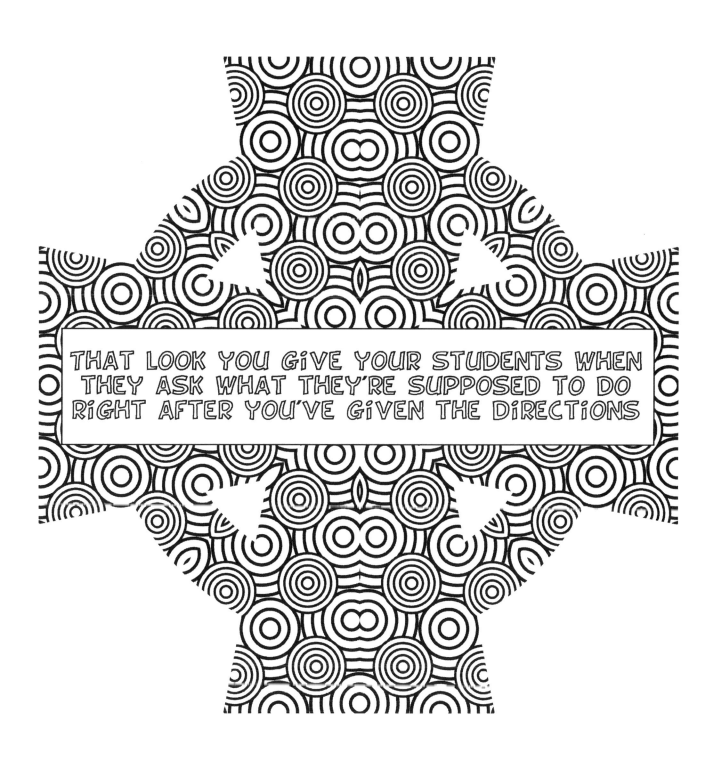

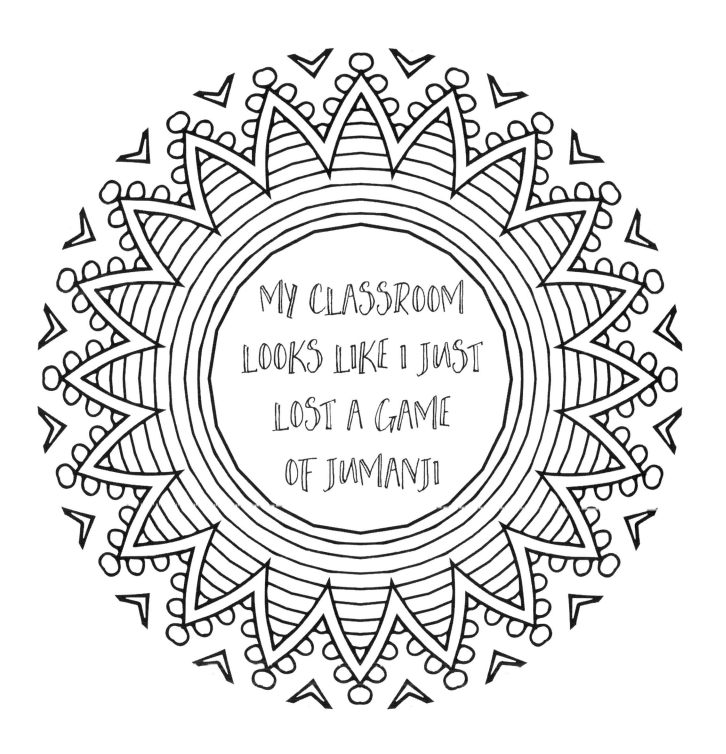

MY CLASSROOM LOOKS LIKE I JUST LOST A GAME OF JUMANJI

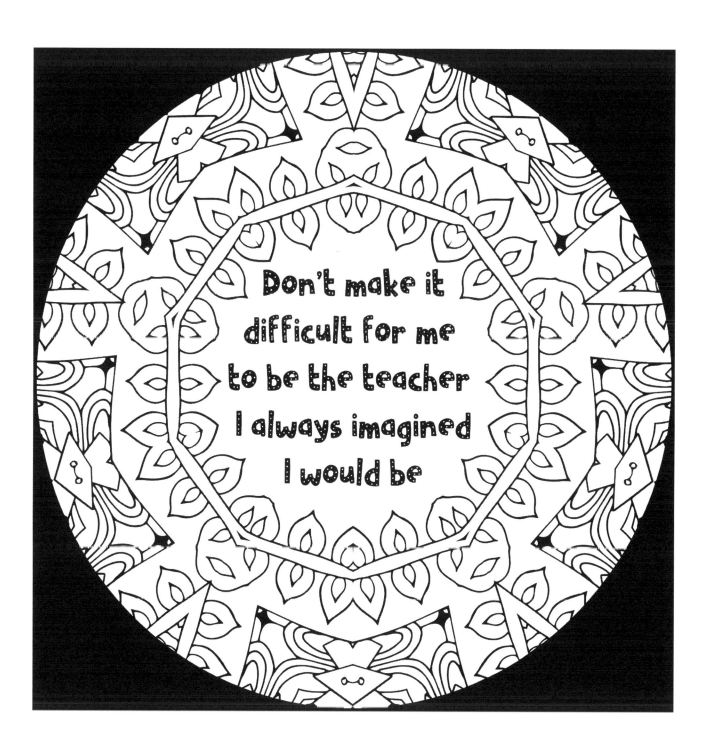

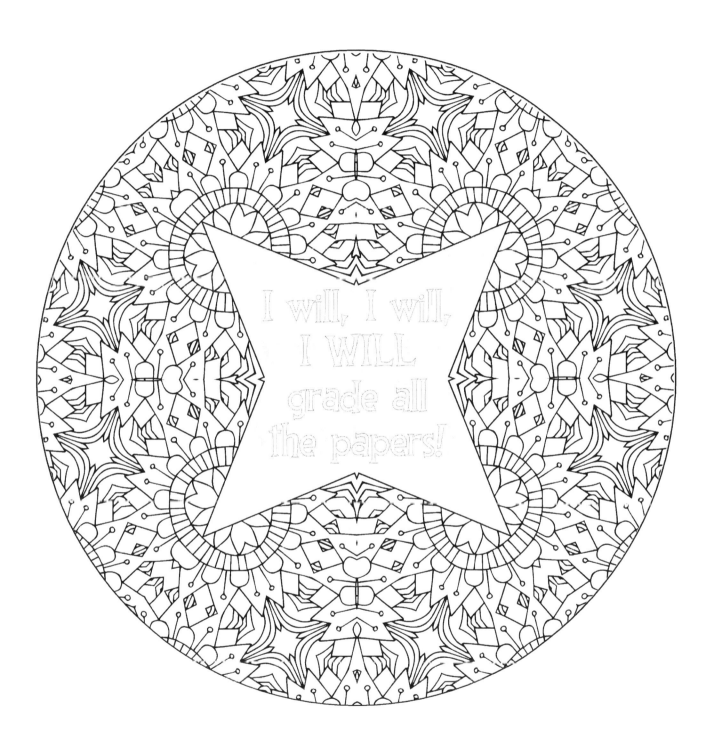

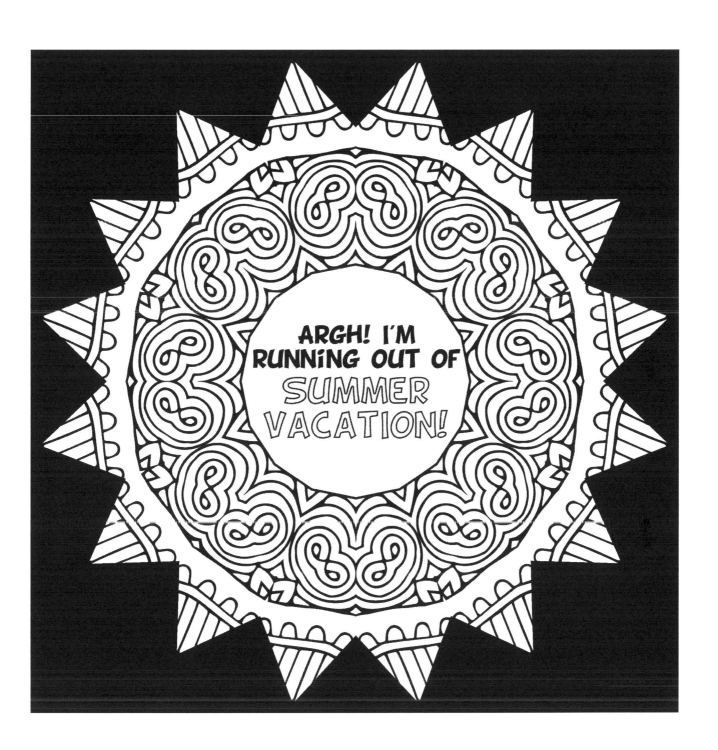

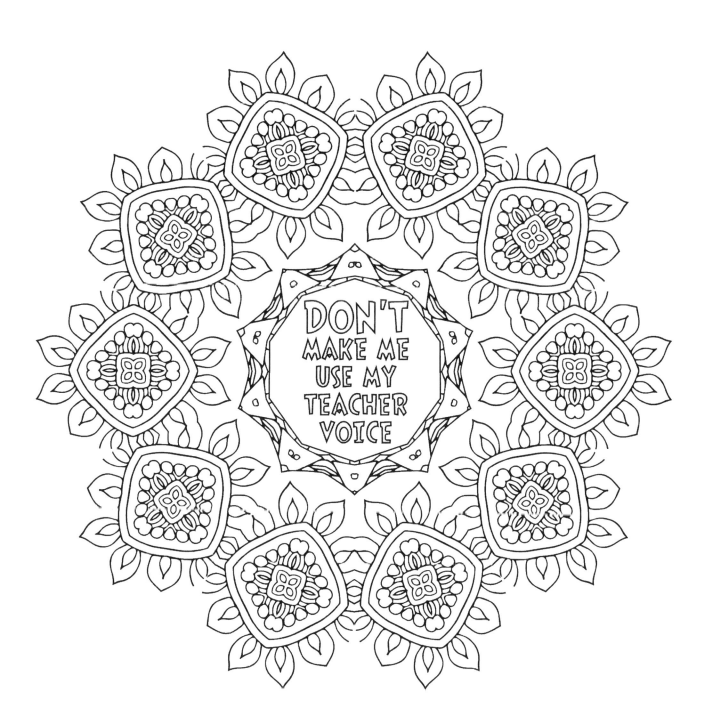

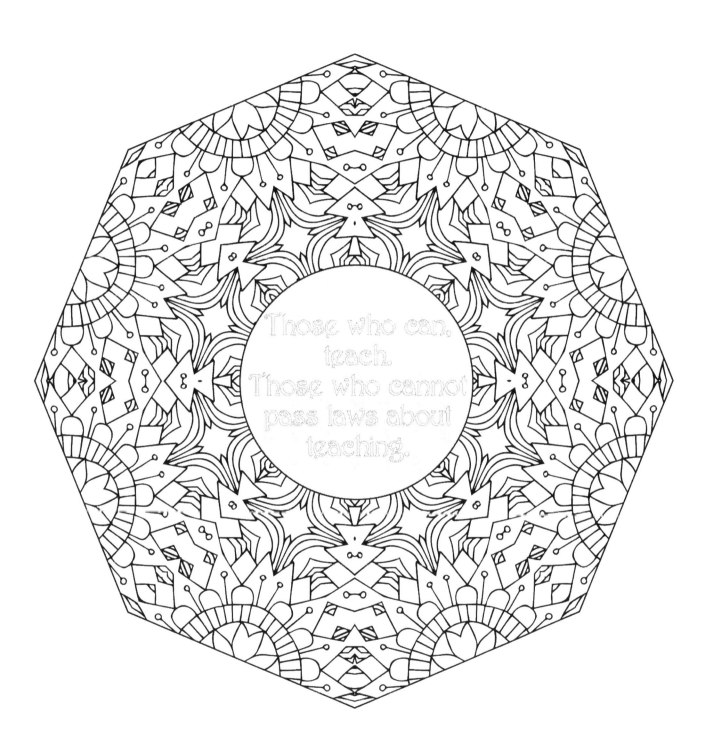

Those who can,
teach.
Those who cannot
pass laws about
teaching.

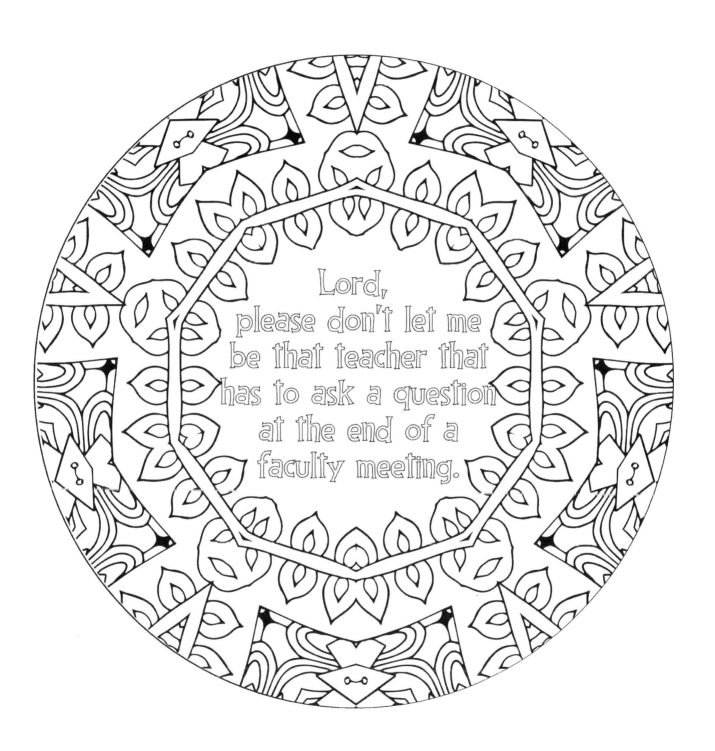

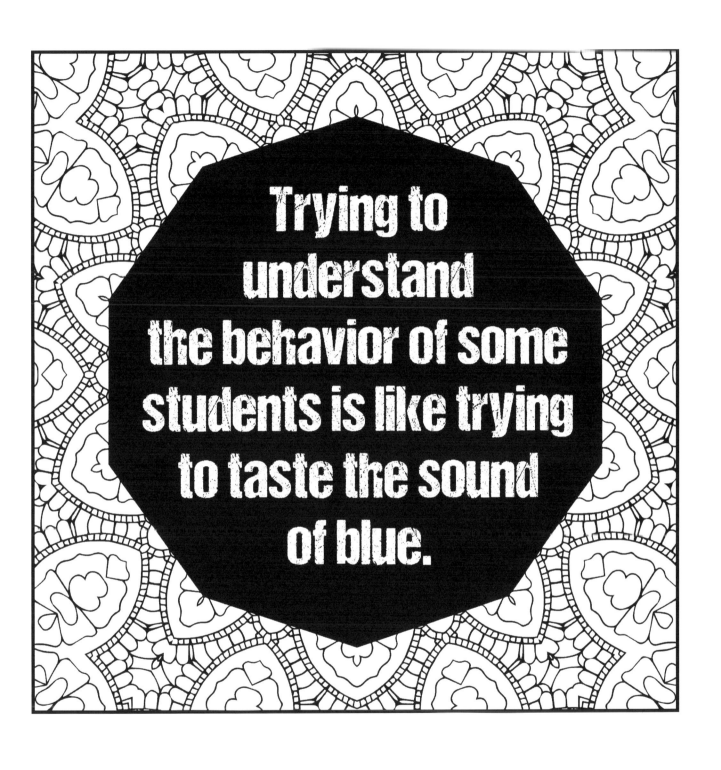

Trying to understand the behavior of some students is like trying to taste the sound of blue.

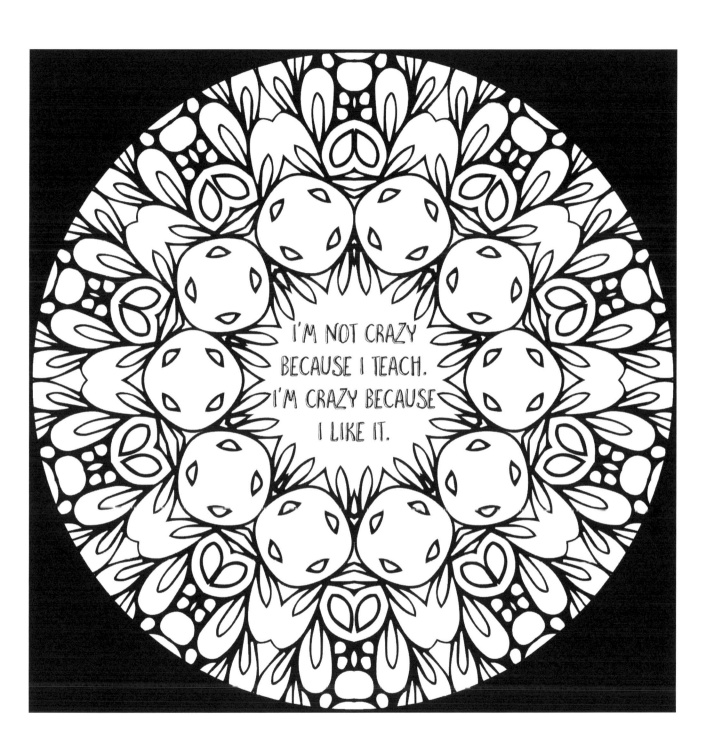

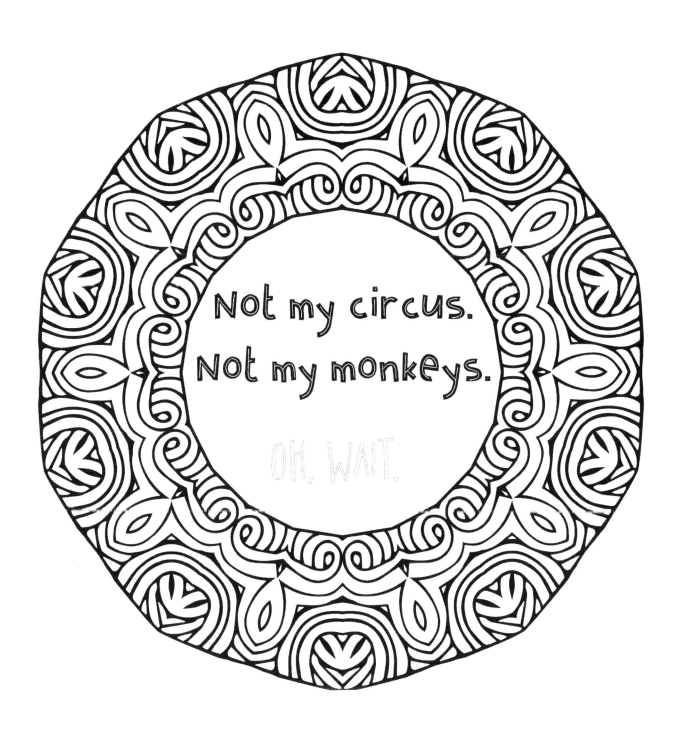

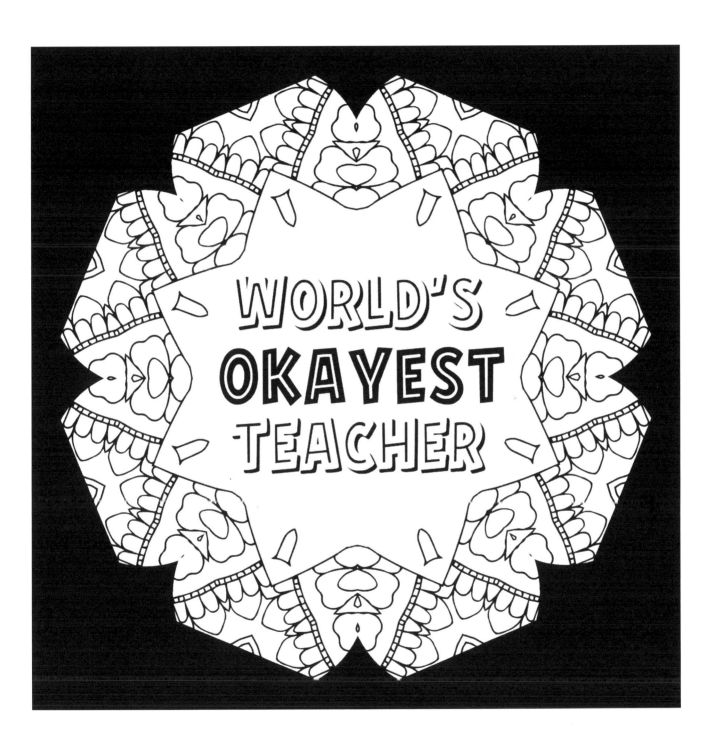

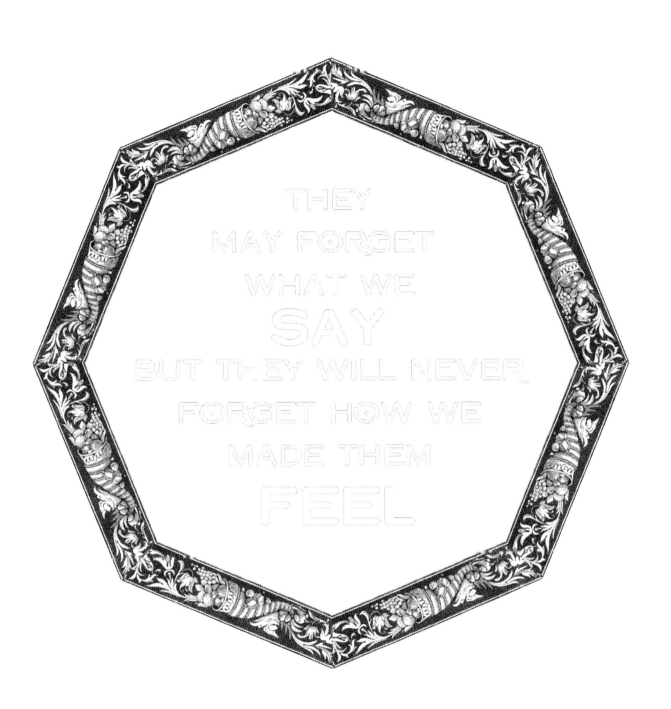

THEY
MAY FORGET
WHAT WE
SAY
BUT THEY WILL NEVER
FORGET HOW WE
MADE THEM
FEEL

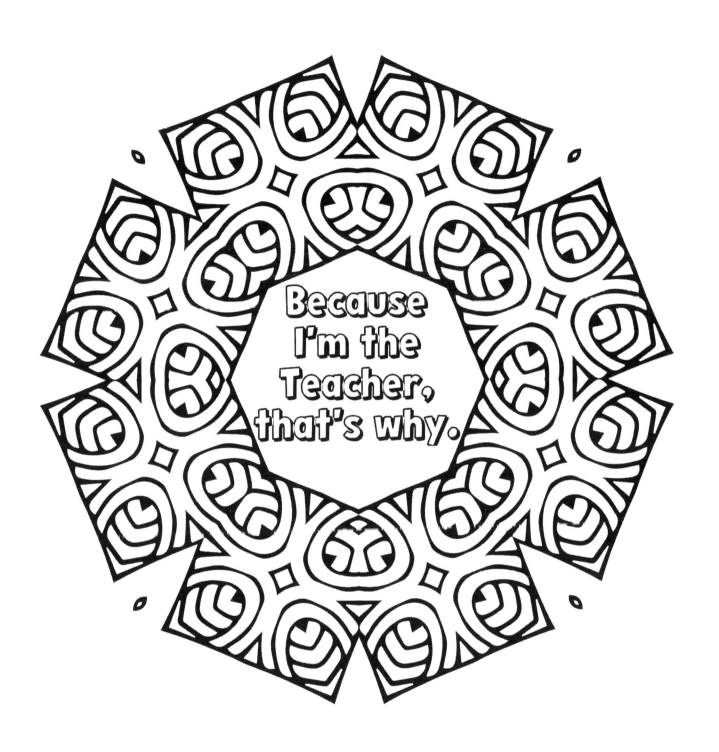

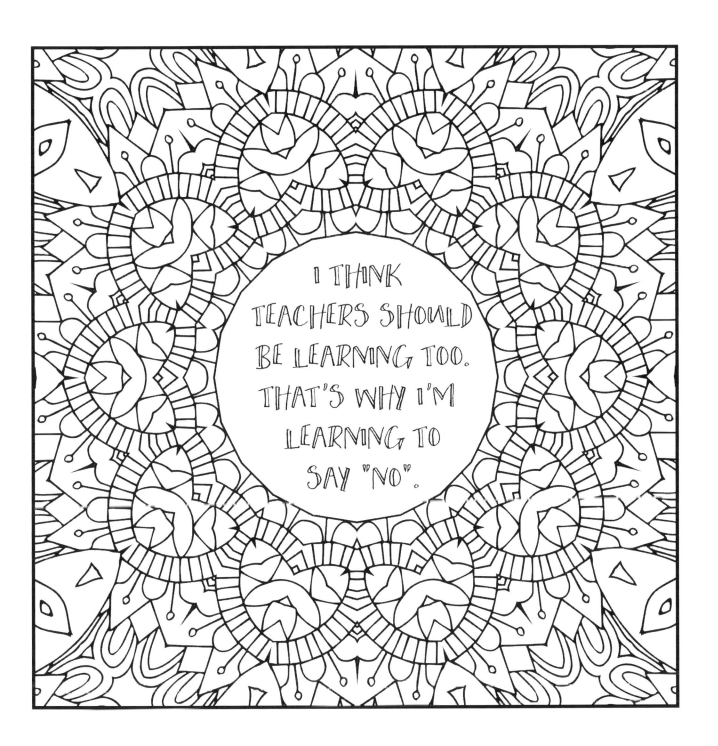

I THINK TEACHERS SHOULD BE LEARNING TOO. THAT'S WHY I'M LEARNING TO SAY "NO".

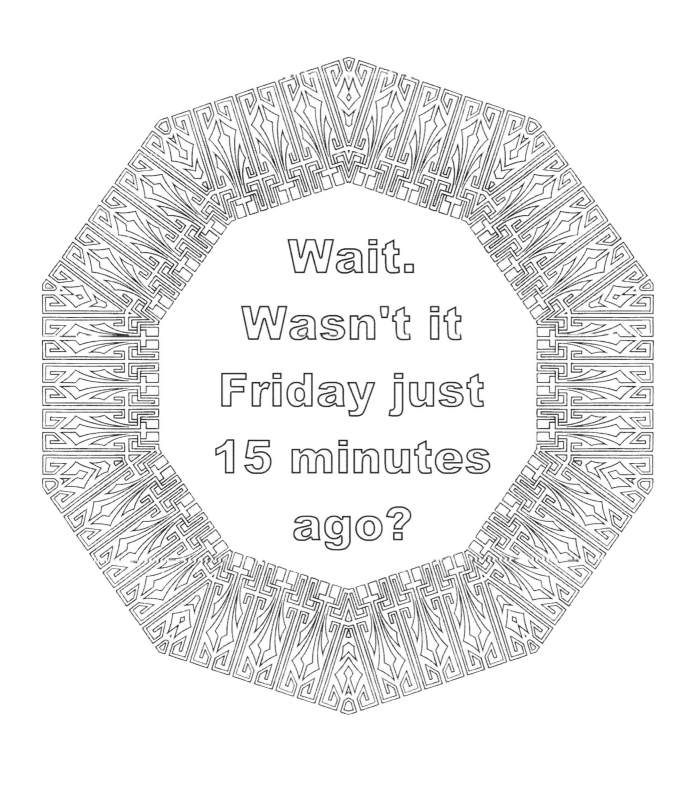

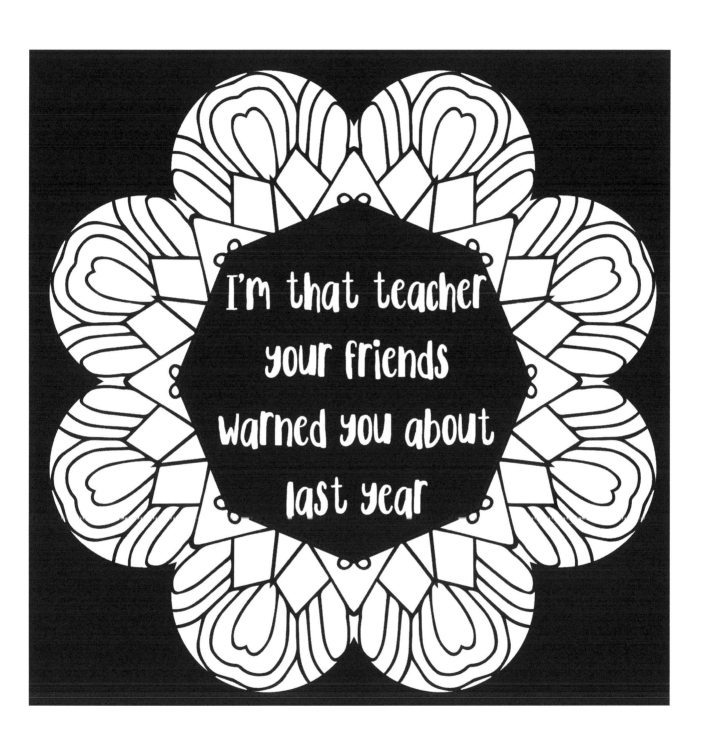

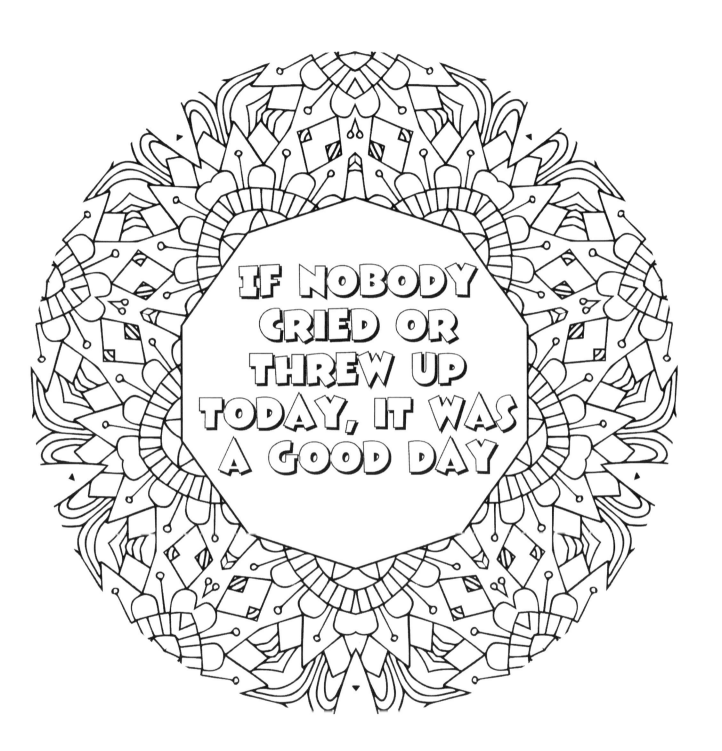

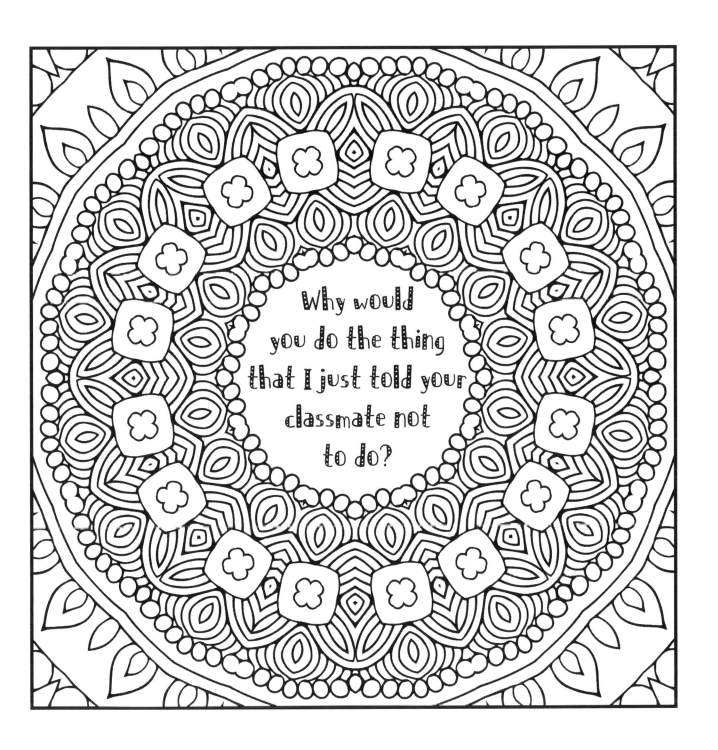

Why would you do the thing that I just told your classmate not to do?

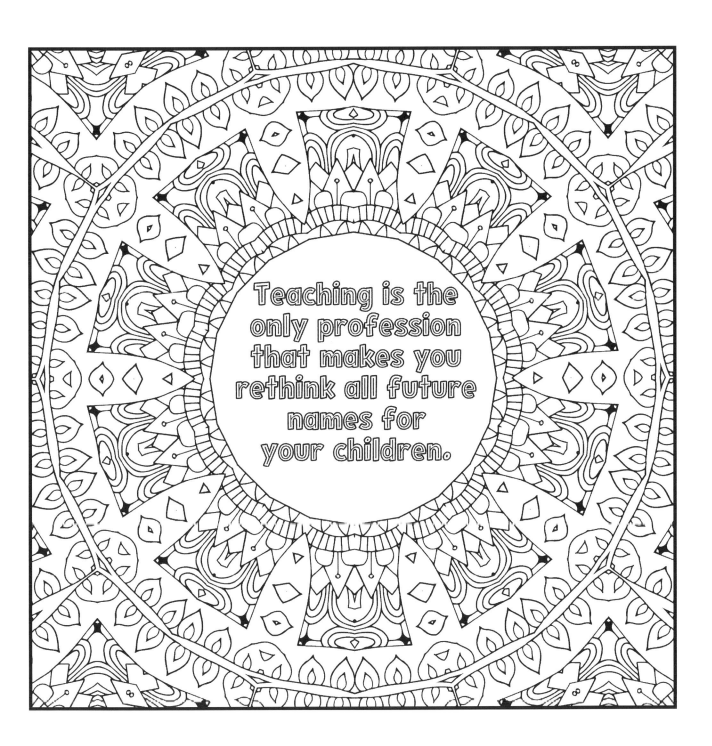

I WON'T BELIEVE EVERYTHING YOUR KIDS SAY ABOUT WHAT HAPPENS AT YOUR HOME...

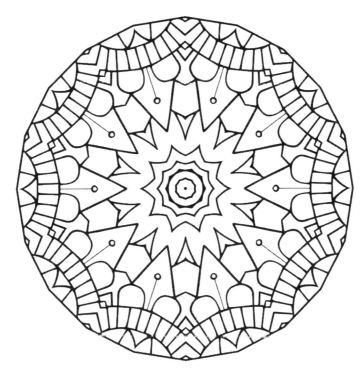

IF YOU WON'T BELIEVE EVERYTHING THEY SAY ABOUT WHAT HAPPENS IN MY CLASS

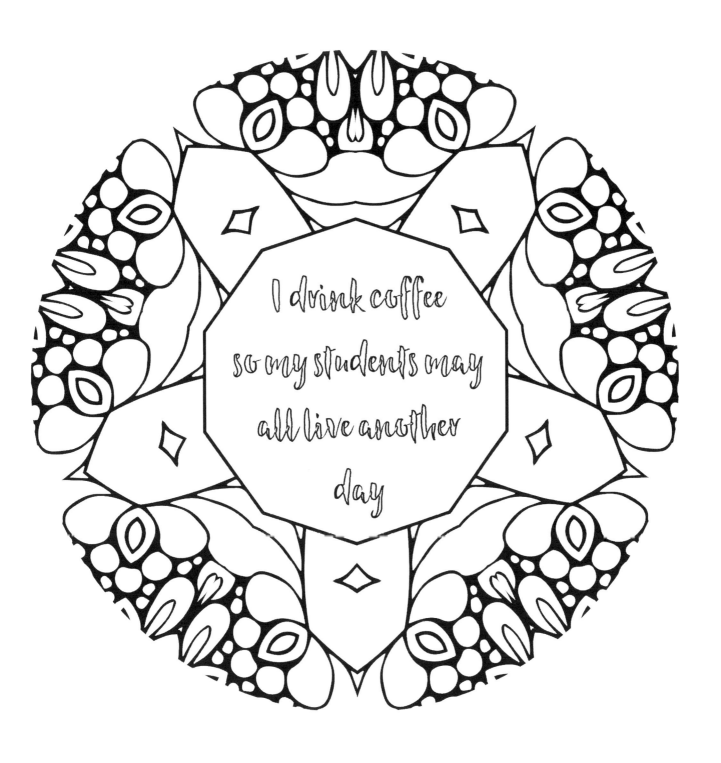

I drink coffee
so my students may
all live another
day

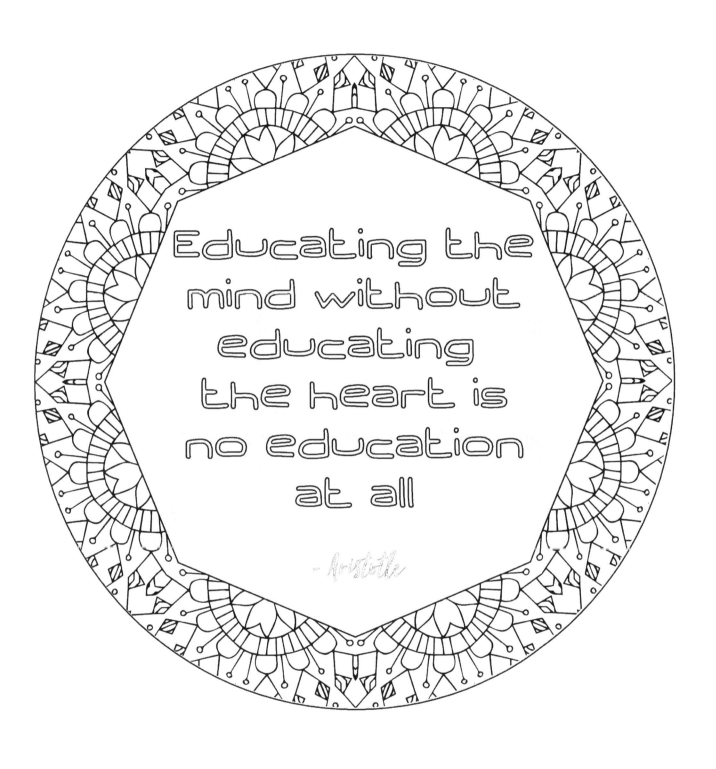

Educating the
mind without
educating
the heart is
no education
at all

- Aristotle

Made in the USA
Middletown, DE
22 February 2017